THOMAS EDISON
WINTER ESTATE

THOS. A. EDISON
HOME
FORT MYERS, FLA.

THOMAS EDISON

Edison began experimenting at an early age, encouraged by his mother. He obtained his first patent at the age of 21, an electric vote counter designed for use in Congress. He married his first wife, Mary Stilwell on Christmas Day in 1871; she died in 1884. They had three children: Marion - 1873, Thomas - 1876, William - 1878.

In 1885 Edison and a long time friend, Ezra Gilliland, came to Florida because of Edison's health. The purchase of the property and the erection of the two homes was a joint venture by Edison and Gilliland; Edison bought Gilliland's house in 1906 and used it as a guest house. The cottage pictured below was on the site when Edison bought the property.

Edison married Mina Miller, from Akron, Ohio in February of 1886, and they came to Fort Myers for their honeymoon. The couple had three children; Madeline - 1888, Charles - 1890, Theodore - 1898.

Thomas and Mina Edison - ca 1900

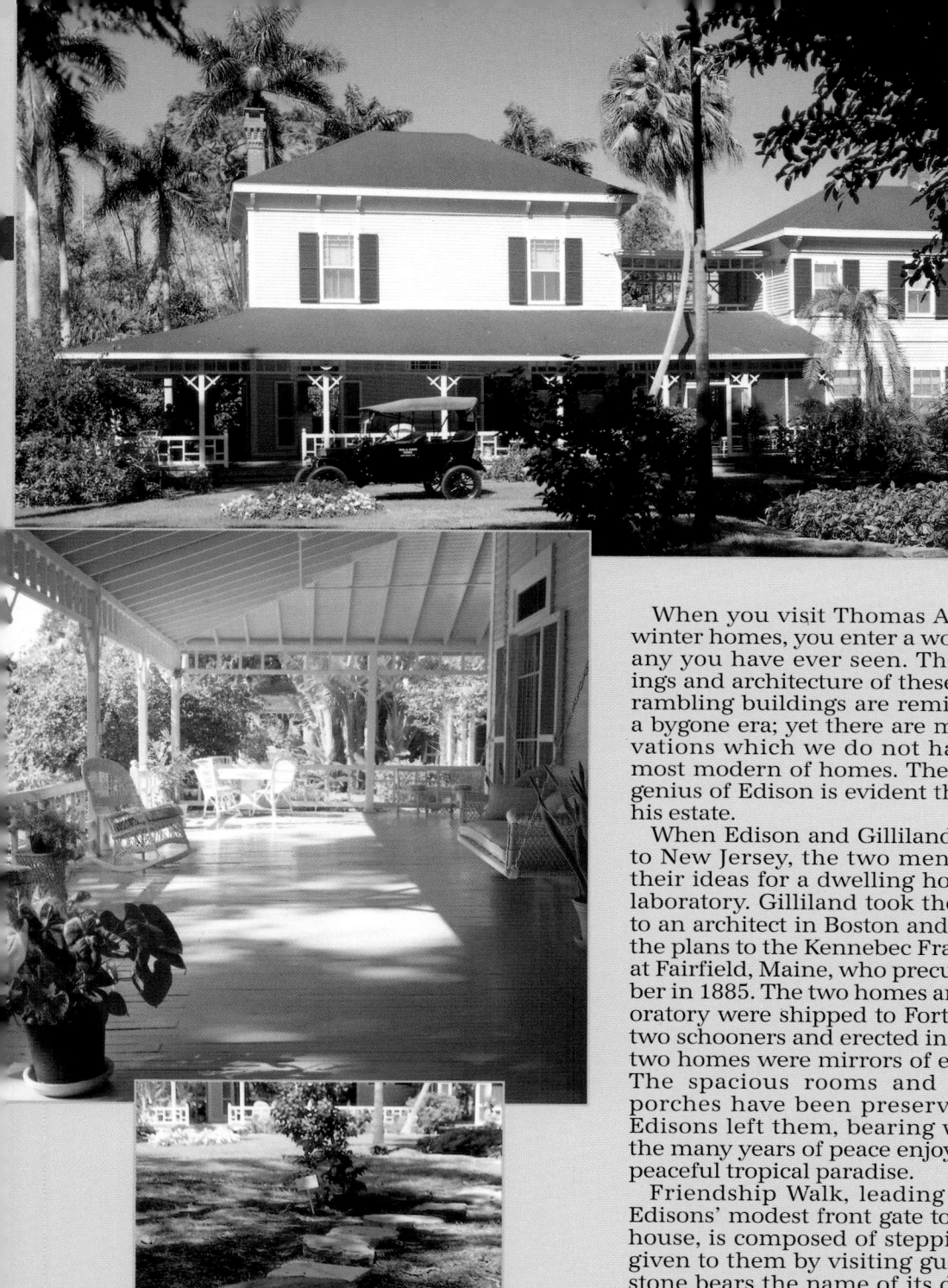

When you visit Thomas A. Edison's winter homes, you enter a world unlike any you have ever seen. The furnishings and architecture of these gracious, rambling buildings are reminiscent of a bygone era; yet there are many innovations which we do not have in the most modern of homes. The inventive genius of Edison is evident throughout his estate.

When Edison and Gilliland returned to New Jersey, the two men sketched their ideas for a dwelling house and a laboratory. Gilliland took the sketches to an architect in Boston and then sent the plans to the Kennebec Framing Co., at Fairfield, Maine, who precut the lumber in 1885. The two homes and the laboratory were shipped to Fort Myers by two schooners and erected in 1886. The two homes were mirrors of each other. The spacious rooms and generous porches have been preserved as the Edisons left them, bearing witness to the many years of peace enjoyed in this peaceful tropical paradise.

Friendship Walk, leading from the Edisons' modest front gate towards his house, is composed of stepping stones given to them by visiting guests. Each stone bears the name of its donor and often includes the date given. Here walked such famous names as Harvey Firestone, Henry Ford, John Burroughs.

"There is no substitute for hard work."

Thomas Edison

3

A portrait of Mina Edison graces the fireplace wall in the Edisons' living room, which is furnished with their much-loved wicker, a popular style in the 1920's. The doors opened on to the spacious verandas of the home and the connected guest house and provided cooling ventilation when needed.

The ten handmade brass chandeliers, Electroliers, throughout the homes came from Mr. Edison's home at Menlo Park, no two alike. They were made in 1880. Each is lighted by the early carbon type filament bulbs. Some of these bulbs, powered by 110 volts, have been burning for some time. They stand in mute homage to Edison's genius for introducing the modern age of light in 1879. On most of the bulb's bases is engraved the symbol 15 c.p., which stands for 15 candle power, equal to approximately a 35 watt bulb of today.

"Life's most soothing things are a child's goodnight and sweet music."

Thomas Edison

The dining room with its early American style furnishings, hand painted china and silver tea service, is exactly as the Edisons left it. The peacock mounted above the door was a family pet while the Edisons were in residence. Note the switch hanging from the lighting fixture. There are no interior light switches in the dining room. This room served as a gathering place of the Edisons and their many famous guests and friends including the Harvey Firestones, the Henry Fords, John Burroughs and President Herbert Hoover.

The turkey platter, designed by Theodore Davis artist-correspondent for Harper's Weekly at the request of the wife of President Hayes, is one piece of an entire assortment of serving pieces produced by Haviland China in 1879. Matching turkey platters may be seen at the White House and the Smithsonian Institute.

5

"A man's best friend is a good wife."

Thomas Edison

Edison had hearing problems early in his life and underwent major surgery on his left ear in 1905 and 1908. As a result of the operations, his ability to hear clearly deteriorated. He had patents with the acoustic telegraph; this helped him to understand the theory of the telephone. His experiments were helpful in making the telephone a successful and beneficial invention. He had a special receiver in the phone to make it easier for him to hear.

Below is the bedroom of Mr. and Mrs. Edison. Note the red brick fireplace; the entire home was heated by this method; there are fireplaces in many of the rooms. Edison often sat in this bedroom and read a number of newspapers every day. He was a speed reader, and his memory was phenomenal. In his office in West Orange, there is a huge library that contains over 10,000 books. As a telegrapher he developed excellent hand writing.

During World War I, Edison was Chairman of the U.S. Navy Consulting Board, helping to develop devices for protecting ships from torpedoes as well as manufacturing vital chemicals relating to the war. He recommended a Naval Research Laboratory, which was established by an act of Congress in 1920. It was placed in Washington, DC.

In 1925, Henry Ford convinced Edison to let him take the laboratory that Edison erected in 1886 to Dearborn, Michigan in 1928. The laboratory was built the same way as the two homes in 1886, pre-cut. In 1929, Mrs. Edison had a small office and garden erected on the site of the old laboratory as a surprise. The office is surrounded with a memory garden complete with blooming plants such as Star Jasmine, and Bougainvillea. The chimney is graced with Queen's Wreath.

Among Florida's first modern swimming pools, was this one built by Edison in 1910. It is constructed of Edison Portland Cement, for which he had 40 patents dealing with its development and production. He built the seven foot deep pool for the entertainment of his children and guests. For himself, Edison felt mental exercise was the only type needed. Edison is responsible for the invention of the "long Kiln," still used in making cement today. Yankee Stadium and the underwater portions of the Panama Canal were built using Edison cement. He is also credited with providing the material for the first cement highway. Testimony to Edison's fine product is the fact that his swimming pool has never developed a leak.

The waterproof electric switch, still in use at the pool and on porches, is another Edison invention.

The Edison Winter Estate is located on the banks of the Caloosahatchee River. This river originates in Lake Okeechobee and empties into the Gulf of Mexico 14 miles to the west of the estate.

The warm waters of this river provide moisture for the gardens and plantings on the estate. Edison had a dock erected which projected 1500 feet into the wide river. It is from this dock that he unloaded his pre-cut houses and endless quantities of chemicals and laboratory equipment. A boat house protected his electric launch, the "Reliance." Both were destroyed in a hurricane some years ago.

Mina Edison adored birds. She kept cages of canaries, parakeets and parrots outdoors year round and placed bird houses in the river to prevent the neighborhood cats from harming her feathered friends.

In 1886, Edison placed electric standards throughout the grounds of his estate powered by a system of underground cables. The electric lights were not turned on until March 27, 1887. For Fort Myers it was a history-making event, and almost everyone in town wandered out to Edison's home that evening to witness the miracle of science.

Edison's Laboratory

> "The only time I become discouraged is when I think of all the things I like to do and the little time I have in which to do them."
>
> *Thomas Edison*

Edison worked long hours in his laboratories, totally unaware of the time, eating when he was hungry and taking "cat naps" in the workshop as needed. He is quoted as having said, "I owe my success to the fact that I never had a clock in my workroom." He also said that his deafness was an asset, explaining that it allowed him to work with less distraction and to sleep deeply, undisturbed by outside sounds. Another secret of Edison's was his unfailing curiosity and unlimited patience. "Genius," he said, "is one percent inspiration and ninety nine percent perspiration." Edison's powerful imagination, firm optimism, self-confidence, and persistence allowed him to complete the numerous experiments which added up to 1,093 U.S. patents, more than any single individual. The Edison laboratory built in 1928 still contains his early laboratory apparatus: a darkroom for developing film, stills for processing goldenrod rubber, and early machinery.

After World War I there was a surplus of rubber, and the price fell to 16 cents per pound in 1920. In November of 1922, the British promulgated the Stevenson Rubber Restriction Act. The U.S. consumed over 70% of the world production. By July, 1925, the demand increased because of balloon tires and, the price of rubber shot up to $1.23 per pound.

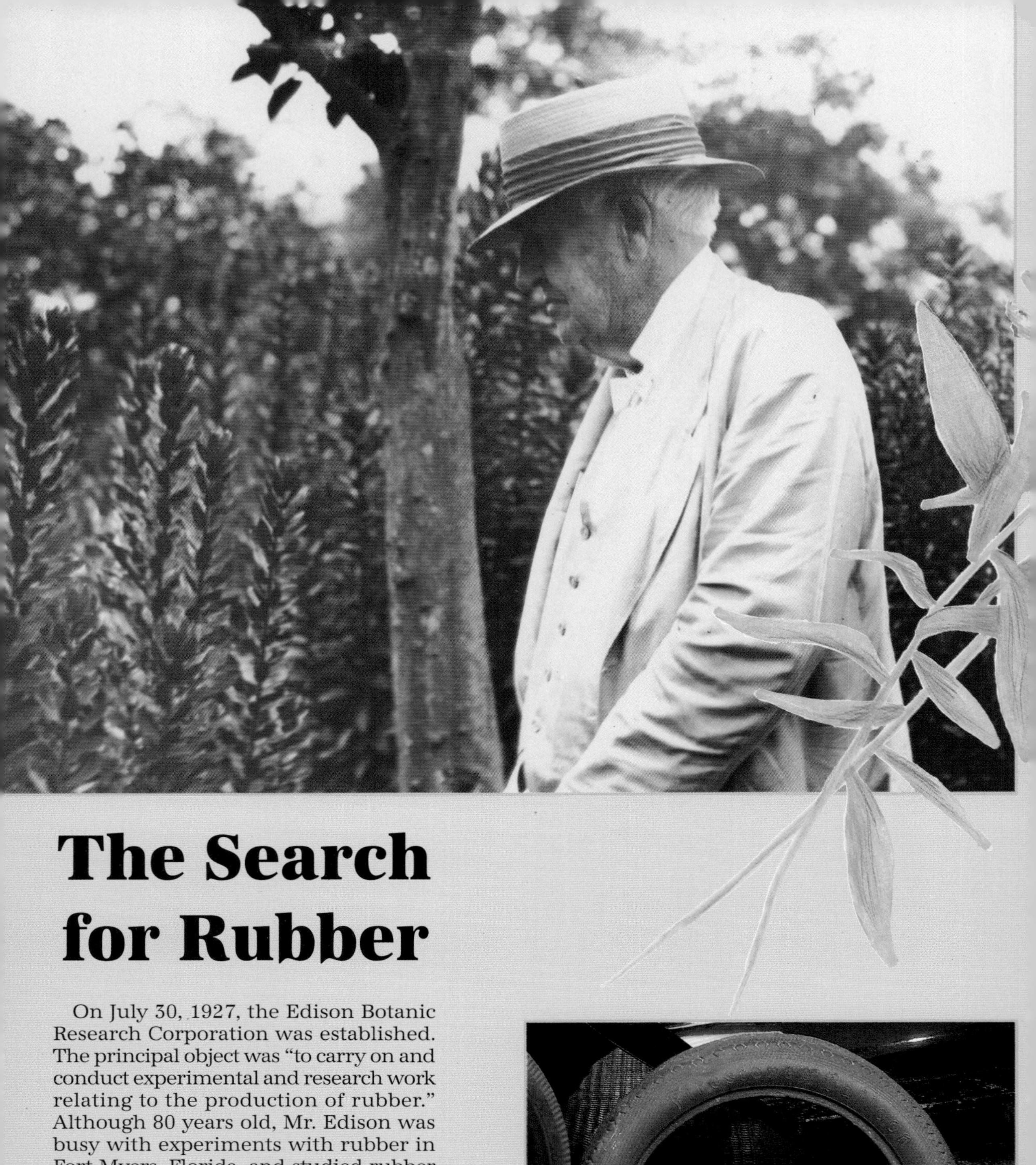

The Search for Rubber

On July 30, 1927, the Edison Botanic Research Corporation was established. The principal object was "to carry on and conduct experimental and research work relating to the production of rubber." Although 80 years old, Mr. Edison was busy with experiments with rubber in Fort Myers, Florida, and studied rubber culture in New York. Edison experimented with thousands of different plants in his search for natural rubber. Edison had a basic philosophy that nature provides answers to problems if one will only seek. His objective was a source of domestic production in the event of an emergency – a plant that would grow rapidly, produce more than one crop a year, and which could be harvested and processed largely by machinery.

TIRE MADE FROM GOLDEN-ROD RUBBER FORMERLY ON EDISON'S MODEL 'T' FORD

Solidago or the goldenrod plant, is a common weed found throughout North America. In the wild, the plant grows two to four feet high on slender stems topped with long plumes of golden blossoms. Once Edison discovered the plant's rubber content, he created a fertilization and cultivation process that soon produced plants averaging 142 inches tall and yielding as much as 12 percent rubber. The rubber produced through Edison's process was resilient and long lasting. Examples of it may still be found in his laboratory, elastic and rot free after more than 50 years. Edison's work with goldenrod rubber was turned over to the government about 1930 and, after his death in 1931, some of his employees continued to conduct research at the facility until 1936. Despite Edison's efforts and those of several government agencies, goldenrod rubber never traveled beyond the experimental stage.

The chemical laboratory has been preserved as Edison left it. The test tubes, bottles and apparatus remain set out on tables as if awaiting the genius' return.

"Until man duplicates a blade of grass, nature can laugh at his so-called scientific knowledge."

Thomas Edison

Edison's Botanical Garden

In the photograph at the right, Edison and his wife are seen strolling the botanical garden some time in the 1920's. The Edison's garden flourishes over most of the 14 acre estate and contains many unusual specimens of tropical and sub-tropical plantings. Edison himself planted much of the gardens during a span from 1886 to 1930. There are trees from all over the world including specimens from China, Japan, India, Africa, Java, Panama, Mexico and Australia. Many of the trees were planted in Edison's later years as he became increasingly interested in horticulture and botany. He was constantly experimenting with them to discover what products and by-products might be obtained. There are also a number of varieties of rubber trees and plants on the estate which Edison used to conduct his rubber research in his chemical laboratory. The botanical gardens are perhaps the oldest and most complete in the Southeast and are maintained by the City of Fort Myers, to whom the estate was deeded in 1947 upon the death of Mina Edison.

There are a number of graceful stands of native giant bamboo within the gardens. This plant, which grows wild along the banks of the Caloosahatchee River, attracted Edison because after hundreds of experiments he found that carbonized bamboo produced the best filament.

The climate, lush trees, flowers, and bamboo all contributed to why Edison purchased the property. All of them combined together caused Edison to build the homes and a laboratory. The many winters that Edison spent in Fort Myers are ample evidence that he loved and enjoyed his frequent sojourns.

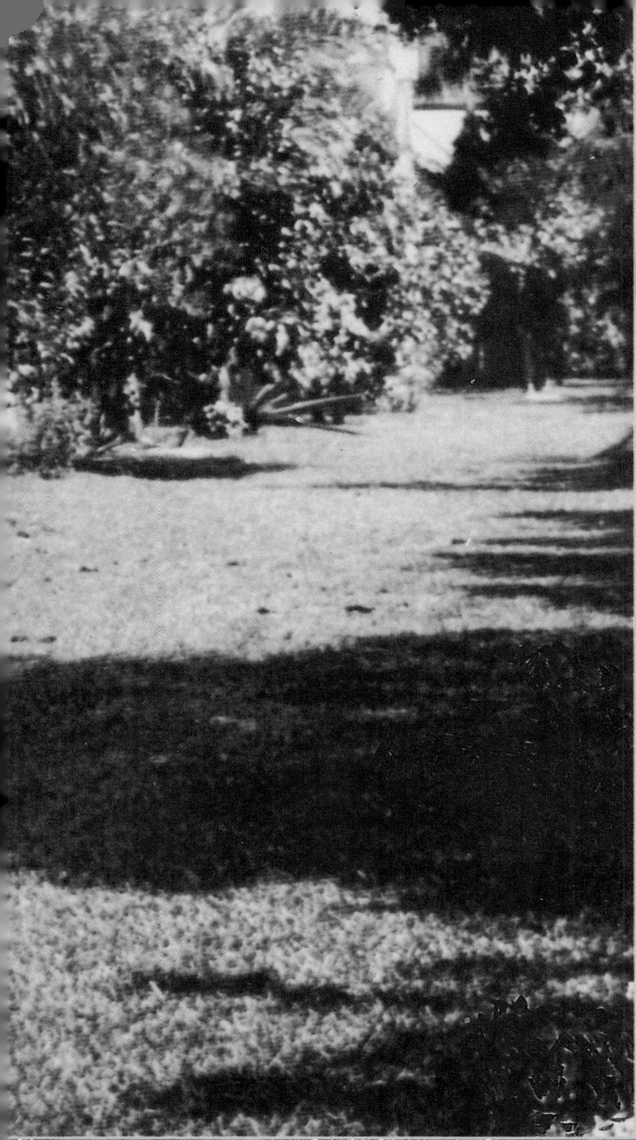

“All progress, all success, springs from thinking.”

Thomas Edison

Perhaps one of the most unusual rubber trees on the Edison Estate is the Moreton Bay Fig or Ficus Macrophylla which grows between the estates of Edison and Henry Ford. This giant specimen, Australia’s national tree, has unusual serpentine roots which extend as far as 200 feet out from the trunk along the surface of the ground. The tree is also referred to as the serpentine fig. Another unusual specimen transplanted from Australia is the Coccoloba Grandifalia or Australian Seagrape. This tree has huge green leaves, often 40 inches in diameter, and thrives in Florida’s mild climate.

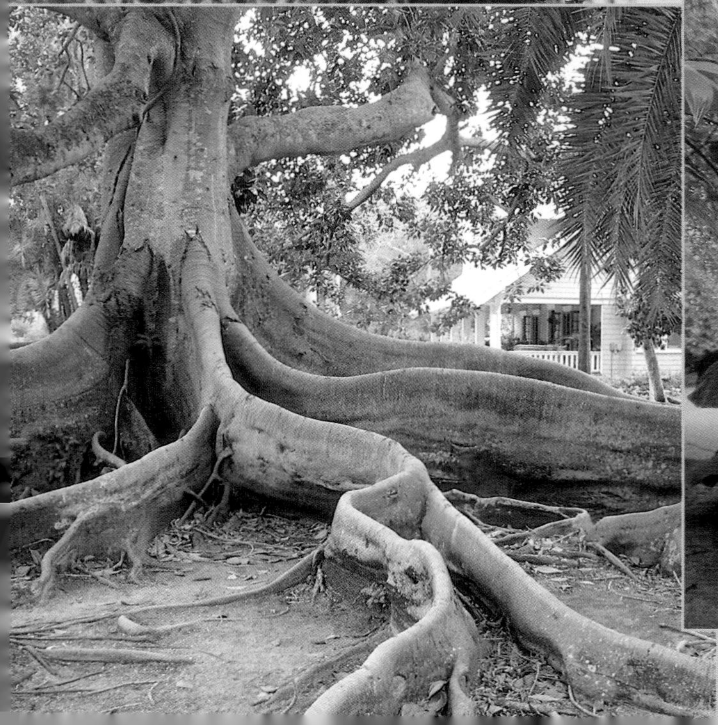

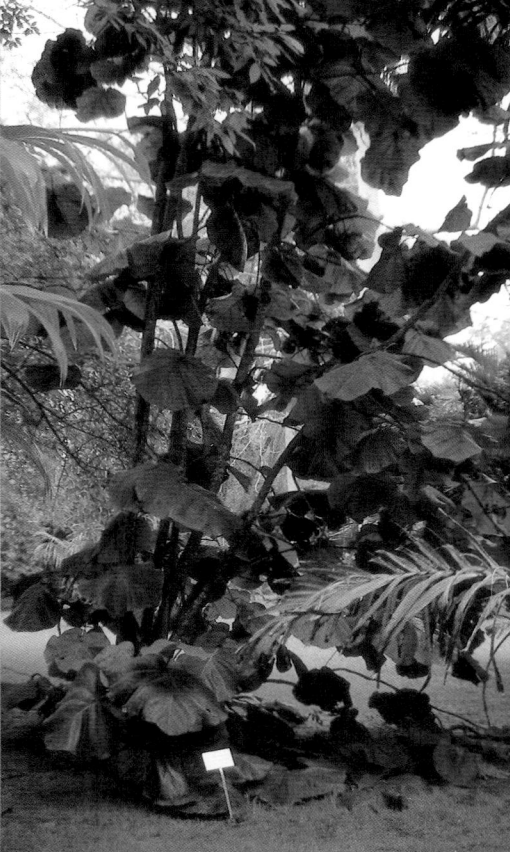

(INDIA, **BANYAN TREE** (S.E. ASIA)
FICUS BENGALENSIS)
Given to Edison by Firestone in 1925
Circumference of Aerial Roots: 390 ft.

17

The Edison botanical gardens are a glorious mixture of flowering plants and trees, many of which produce wonderful exotic fruits. The beautiful blue flowering vine which graces the chimney of Edison's office is the Petrea or Queen's Wreath. This showy vine flowers during the summer months and is a native of Brazil.

Several varieties of bananas are among the fruits grown in the gardens and may be seen ripening, turning from brilliant green to glorious yellow, nearly all year round. There are over 50 different varieties of fruits grown in the garden including mangos, a native of India. Of all the trees transplanted to the Edison Estate, the mango tree provides the best host for wild native Florida orchids as well as cattleyas which can be seen blooming throughout the gardens.

Flowering Trees

The golden rain tree is one of the many yellow flowering trees on the estate. Not only is the flower of this tree spectacular, the seed pod which follows is just as showy with its dark red color. The tree blooms in the summer and is native to China. It seeds prolifically and is as at home in Florida's native soil as it was in the Far East.

The golden chalice vine has large yellow-white bell shaped flowers and is a native of Mexico. It puts on its beautiful show each summer for visitors just as it did for Thomas and Mina.

The botanical gardens, like almost everything Edison did, served several purposes. The fruits provided a glorious harvest, the blooming plants colored and perfumed the air and, perhaps most important of all to Edison, the many plantings provided him with the materials necessary for extensive botanical experimentation.

Exotic Plants

Other specimens of exotic plants in the Edison garden include the Mysorensis, a tall rubber tree with round spatula-like leaves. Edison, through his extensive experiments, decided that this tree and the Ficus Elastica were the only viable sources of natural rubber among the varieties grown in North America. The shrub with the long red tassels is called the Chenille Plant and is native to Bismark Island. Chenille is French for caterpillar, an apt name for this plant's fuzzy flowers.

Edison kept bee hives or "grass skeps" in the gardens. This style of hive is said to have been imported from Holland and was Edison's choice due to his Dutch background. The bees served many purposes; providing honey for the home, pollinating the plantings and producing beeswax which Edison used in making his cylinder phonograph records.

The two types of Bougainvillea in the garden, Rosea and Margaret Bacon, were cultivated in Fort Myers by the late James Hendry. Due to the large variety of plantings, the garden is in bloom nearly year round. Among the plantings may also be found Magnolia, Pincushion Trees, the Lipstick Bush, whose tiny red seeds are used to color lipstick and butter, and Bryophyllum or Miracle Leaf Plant, which reproduces by creating tiny new plants along each leaf's edge.

Below: *Beehives*

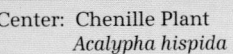

Center: Chenille Plant
Acalypha hispida

Bottom: *Bougainvillea*

Left: Magnolia
Magnolia grandiflora

Below: Pincushion Tree
Nauclea esculenta

"A flower,
a lovely child,
a full-rigged ship
in a stiff breeze
– what is more
beautiful?"

Thomas Edison

Below: Lipstick Plant
Bixa orellana

Above: Miracle Leaf
Bryophyllum Spc.

21

Palm Trees

As the Edison Botanical Garden and its wide variety of trees and plants have matured, the homes, on the banks of the Caloosahatchee River, have become surrounded by their own tropical paradise.

The showy seeds pictured here are from the handsome dwarf cluster palm called Arenga. More than 70 varieties of Palms grow within the gardens.

McGregor Boulevard was once a simple cow path. In 1907, Edison offered to "have royal palms planted on both sides of the road from Manuel's Branch creek to the end of Riverside Avenue in the town, erect proper protection crates, furnish fertilizer and humus for one year from the time of planting, and make any necessary renewals of plants for two years." Today, the palms extend for 15 miles from Fort Myers to Fort Myers Beach gracing this City of Palms.

The Edison Museum

Edison and Ford met for the first time at the 1896 annual meeting of the Association of Edison Illuminating Companies in New York. Ford was working for the Detroit Edison Company; Edison was experimenting with battery cars; Ford, a gas car. At the end of the discussion, Edison banged the table and told Henry "that's the thing, you have it. Your car is self-contained, carries its own power, You have the thing. Keep at it."

In 1916, Ford gave Edison a Model T, and it was modernized frequently by his friend. It was among the first with left-hand steering and a speedometer. The final change was in 1927, when clincher type wheels were replaced with demountable rims and "modern" balloon tires. This automobile was Edison's favorite.

THOS. A. EDISON
HOME
FORT MYERS, FLA.

EDISON'S
MODEL 'T' FORD
PRESENTED TO HIM BY
HIS FRIEND AND NEIGHBOR
HENRY FORD

TIRE MADE FROM
GOLDEN-ROD RUBBER
FORMERLY ON
EDISON'S MODEL 'T' FORD

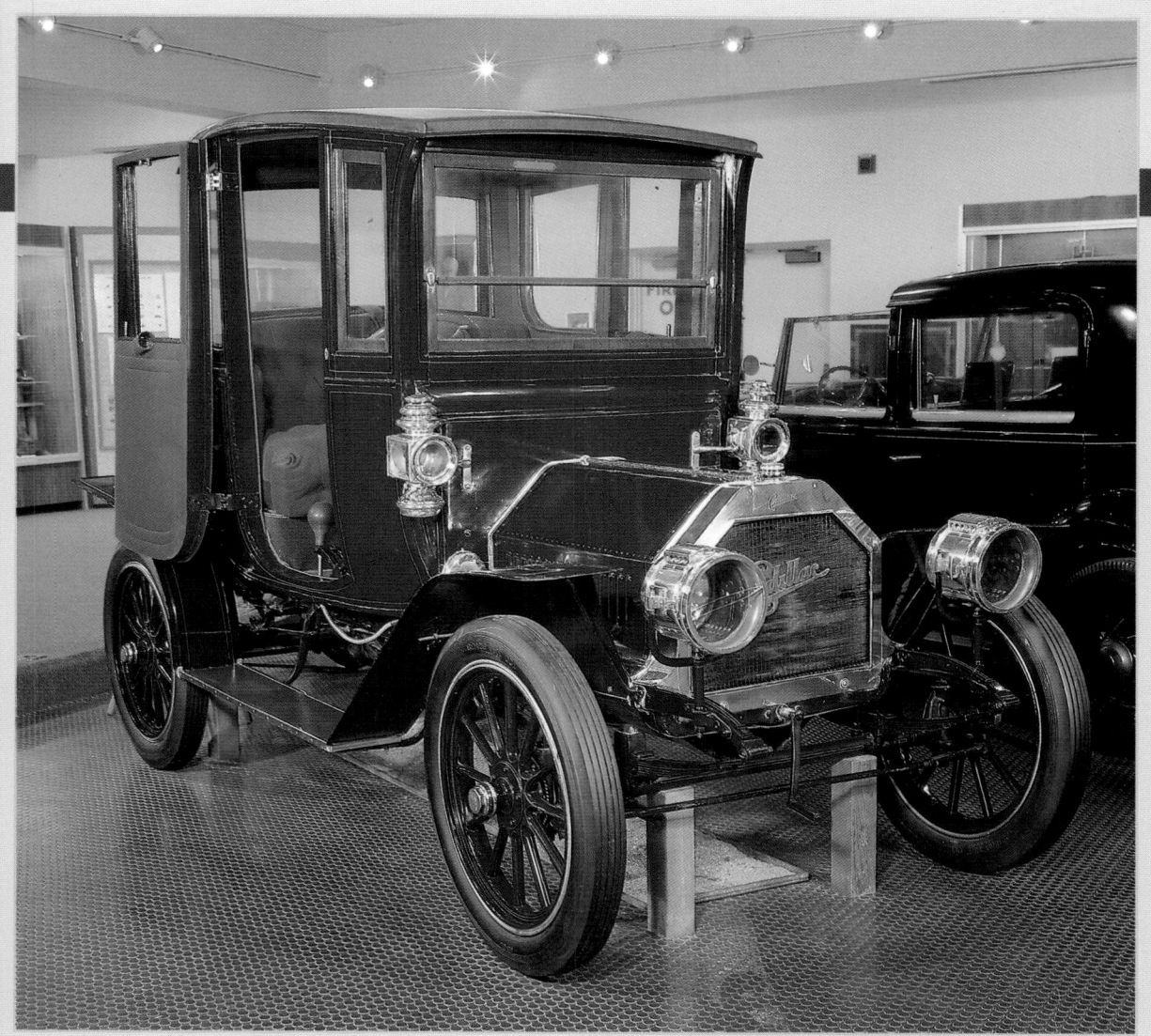

"Friendship is the leaven of life."   Thomas Edison

Edison used his Model "T" as transportation throughout Fort Myers and Lee County. In his later years, Edison loved to go on camping trips in the countryside with his close friends Henry Ford, Harvey Firestone and the great naturalist and bird lover John Burroughs. The four men visited the Everglades and rural Florida towns on many occasions, collecting plants and studying the wildlife, which was abundant at the time. Edison enjoyed studying plants, both native and imported, and incorporated a wide variety of both in his botanical garden. Many of these plants he used in his search for a source of natural rubber. Edison spent much time in his later years in the study of plants.

The automobile pictured above is a 1908 Cadillac. The car was custom made for Edison and is one of a kind. It was built by the Cadillac Company who used the enclosed body chassis of the then Columbia Electric Car Company. The enclosed body style was very useful in the colder northern climate, unlike other models of its time. The automobile has a four cylinder gasoline engine and was donated to the museum by Dr. Samuel Scher of New York City.

Edison experimented with the automobile in his New Jersey "invention factory," using his alkaline storage battery as a source of power instead of the gasoline engine.

THOMAS ALVA EDISON

Age 10 (1857)

1888

With Charles P. Steinmetz, at GE

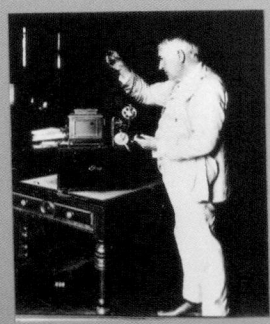

1912

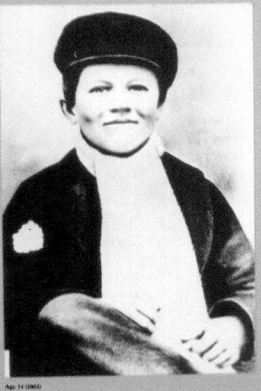

Age 14 (1861)

Some Edison Dates

1847	Born, February 11, in Milan, Ohio
1859-1863	Job selling newspapers and sundries on train between Port Huron, Mich. (new home) and Detroit
1864-1867	Wander-years as a telegrapher
1868	In Boston, first patented invention
1869	In New York, work on stock ticker, printing telegraph
1870	First substantial income from an invention (stock ticker)
1871	Marries Mary Stilwell
1874	Quadruplex telegraph (sending four messages over a wire at the same time)
1876	Carbon-resistance telephone transmitter
1877	Phonograph
1879	Incandescent lamp
1882	Pearl Street station in New York
1883	Discovers Edison Effect (basis of vacuum tube)
1884	Wife Mary dies
18	Marries Mina Miller
188	Newer, larger laboratory at West Orange
1888	Motion pictures
1889-1893	Concentrated activity on electro-magnetic ore-separation work in Ogdenburg, N.J.
1889	More work on phonograph
1889	Development of storage battery
1923	Attempt to find alternate sources of rubber
1929	Inauguration of Menlo Park Laboratory as a museum in Dearborn, Mich.
1931	Dies, October 18, West Orange, N.J.

1930, shortly before his death

Edison's Inventions

The printing telegraph or stockticker with a keyboard of letters was developed by Edison in his Newark factory in 1871. This was one of his early patents and the first one for which he received any money. Edison was asked by the Gold and Stock Telegraph Company how much he wanted for the patent. Instead of asking for the $3,000 to $5,000 he had in mind, he replied, "Make me an offer." He was amazed when they offered and paid him $40,000. With this money he opened a laboratory and built a factory in Newark, New Jersey, where he employed 300 workers and began turning out a number of money-making inventions. One of the first was the Electric Pen in 1877, the forerunner of the mimeograph machine, and the foundation of his life-long friendship with Albert B. Dick. The Embossing Telegraph, pictured below, which vastly increased the speed and accuracy of transmitted messages, was, according to Edison, the father of the phonograph, another of his inventions.

"I find out what the world needs. Then I go ahead and try to invent it."

Thomas Edison

The Phonograph

"Of all my inventions I like the phonograph best."

Thomas Edison

Model of the first phonograph in his laboratory at Menlo Park, New Jersey. Thomas A. Edison sketched the plans for his first phonograph which was made by his assistant John Kruesi.

On December 6th, 1877, Edison recorded the words from the child's nursery rhyme "Mary had a Little Lamb" and this was the first recording of the human voice ever successfully repeated by a mechanical device.

This painting of a charming old couple enthralled with their phonograph is the work of the noted Italian artist Massani. It was imported to New York in 1906 and obtained by the Edison association. A slightly modified version was used extensively to advertise Edison's cylinder phonograph. The painting first appeared in the 1906 issue of the Edison Phonograph Monthly. The original painting was donated to the Edison Estate by Theodore M. Edison, Thomas and Mina's youngest son.

The Edison Amberola Phonograph, pictured at left was introduced in 1913. It played a cylinder record that lasted four minutes. This particular style was called a table model and could be purchased with either a mahogany or golden oak cabinet. Prices for the various models ranged from $65 to $80. These phonographs proved extremely popular due to the fact that they were light weight and easily moved about. Three models were produced, the Amberola 30, 50 and 75, with the 30 being the most popular.

29

"My philosophy of life: work and looking on the bright side of everything."

Thomas Edison

The Edison Phonograph, patented in 1878, was the first actual record player invented and Edison's favorite invention. Years after the invention he said it did for the ears what the motion picture (another of his inventions) did for the eyes and that it put music in people's homes. This is one of the few inventions that worked the first time Edison tried it, a fact that made him skeptical indeed. Edison commercially manufactured the cylinder phonographs from 1895 to 1912, they played both two and four minute cylinder records. Each of the many models manufactured came with a metal or wood horn painted black. It was popular to hand paint flower designs inside the horns which were soon nicknamed Morning Glory Horns.

Talking dolls, not the modern invention you might think, were produced by the Edison Phonograph Toy Manufacturing Company in 1890. A small, hand wound mechanism was placed inside the dolls chest and produced the sound.

In 1905, the first coin operated phonograph, the Multiphone, with multiple selections was introduced. It used an Edison spring motor and had 24 cylinder records operated by depositing a nickel and making a selection. Despite the failure of the company in 1909, the juke box had been born.

Edison's Electric Lamp

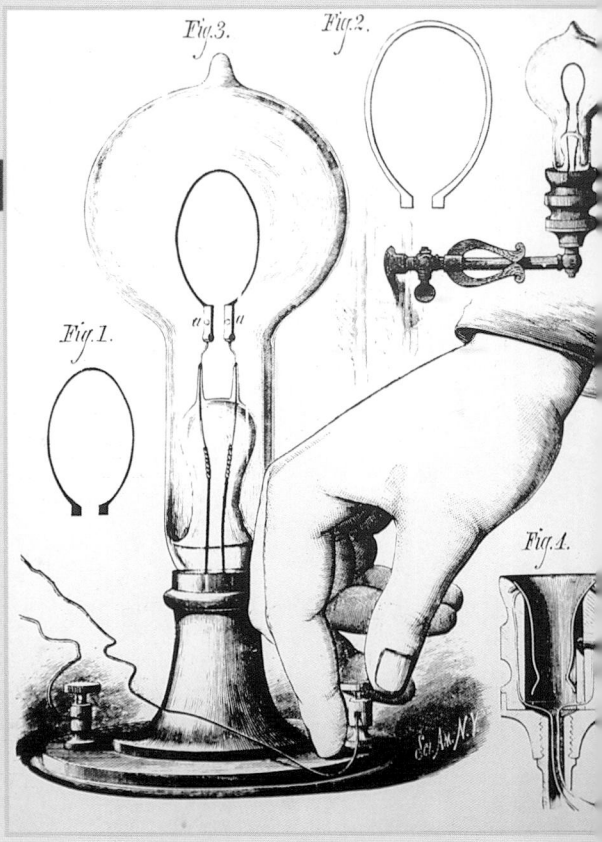

Thomas Edison created the first carbon filament incandescent lamp in 1879. After filling more than 40,000 pages with notes, he finally had a bulb that withstood a 40 hour test in his Menlo Park, NJ laboratory. On December 31 of that year he gave a public demonstration of his electric lighting system in the streets and buildings at Menlo Park. The entire system was interconnected using underground mains. Edison experimented with many materials in his search for a viable filament for his lamp, including human hair and string. He finally settled on carbonized bamboo which increased the life of the bulbs for many hours. This was also the year he established the first incandescent lamp factory at Menlo Park. Edison's discovery introduced the coming of age for mass distribution of electric power.

> ## "I shall make the electric light so cheap that only the rich will be able to burn candles."
>
> ### *Thomas Edison*

Once Edison established his Electric Lamp Company, others joined the rapidly expanding industry in the latter part of the nineteenth century. Joining Edison were entrepreneurs like Brush's arc lamps and dynamos; Wood's "spark-free dynamos" and electric regulation systems; Thomson's and Houston's arc lamps, dynamos, motors, generators, transformers and alternating current power systems; and Sprague's electric street railway systems. Together, they created a revolutionized field of power.

By 1890, Edison had organized his various businesses: the Edison Lamp Company, Edison Machine Works, Edison Electric Tube Company, Edison Shafting Company and the United Edison Manufacturing Company into Edison General Electric Company. The Thomson-Houston Company had also merged with various others. Soon there were two dominant electrical companies, and it became obvious that a merger was in the best interest of both. In 1892, these two major companies combined to form General Electric. However, it was Edison's work between 1878 and 1882 that was the central element in the origins of this great technological transformation.

The General Electric Company

EDISON COMPANIES

1876	1880	1884	1888	1892

Pope, Edison & Co.

Edison Electric Light Co., Menlo Park, N.J.

Edison Lamp Co., Harrison, N.J.

Bergmann & Company, New York City

Edison Machine Works, New York

Edison Electric Tube Company, Brooklyn

Edison Company for Isolated Lighting, New York

Edison Shafting Co. New York City

United Edison Mfg. Co., Schenectady

Sprague Elec. Railway Motor Co., N.Y.

Edison General Electric Company, 1890

THOMSON-HOUSTON COMPANIES

Telegraph Supply Co.

Bush Electric Company Cleveland, Ohio

Van DePoele Elec. Railway Company Chicago

Excelsior Electric Company

American ElectricWorks, New Britain, Conn.

Thomson-Houston Co. Lynn, Mass.

Schuyler Electric Co.

Bentley-Knight Electric Railway Company Cleveland

Thomson-Houston International Electric Co.

GENERAL ELECTRIC COMPANY

1876	1880	1884	1888	1892

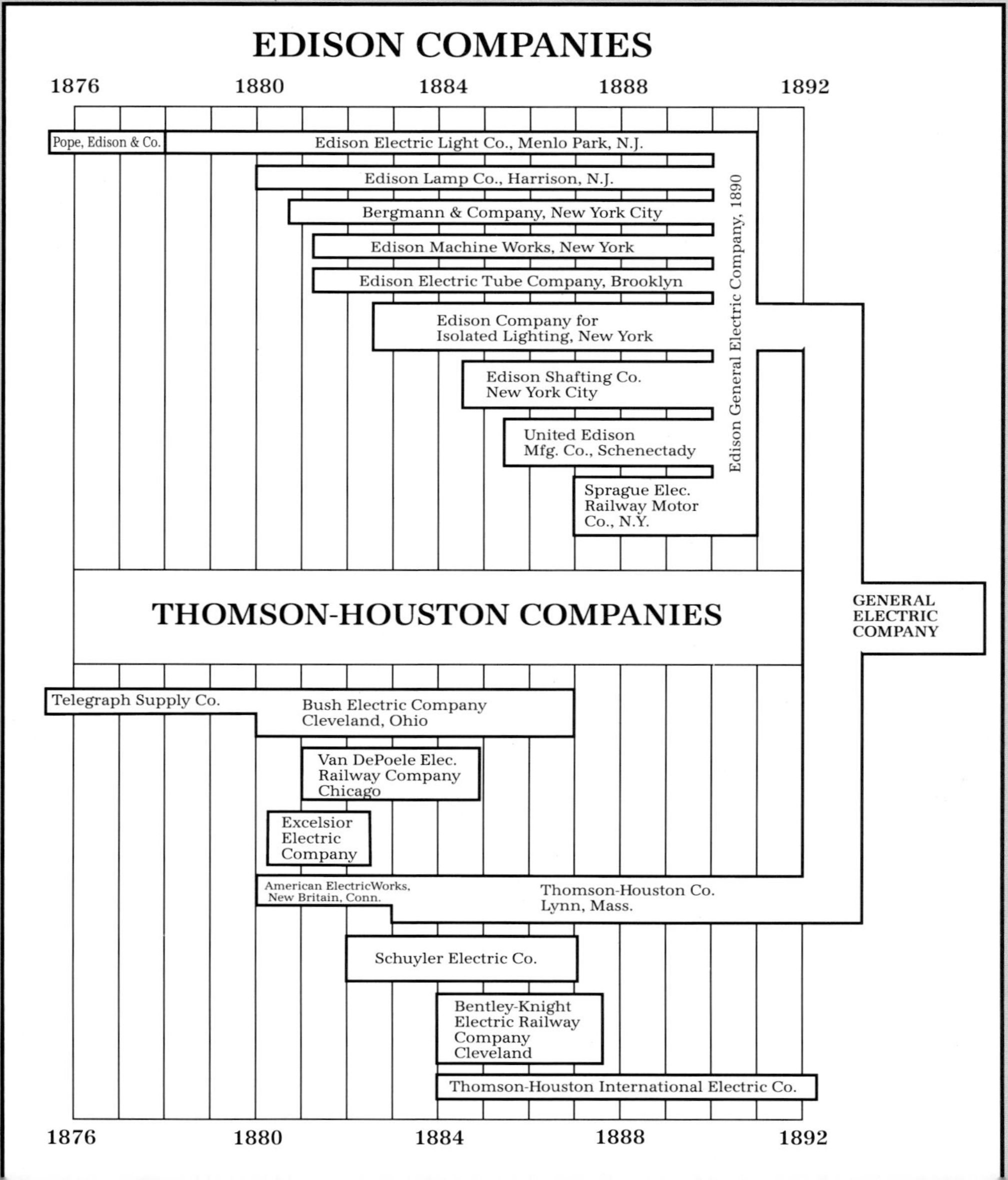

The Early Days of Electric Power

Using the foundations of inventions like Michael Faraday, an English physicist who discovered the principle of converting mechanical energy to electric energy, and generator producers Siemens and Wallace, Edison developed a generator that was 90% efficient. He installed the first three wire system in Sunbury, Pennsylvania and, on July 4, 1883, lit the homes and streets of the village with electricity. Pearl Street Station, *bottom,* was the first incandescent lamp central station in the country. Its six "Jumbo" dynamos supplied 7,200, 16 candle-power lamps over one-sixth of a square mile of New York City.

> "Genius is one per cent inspiration and ninety-nine percent perspiration."
>
> *Thomas Edison*

The Birth of Motion Pictures

In 1887, Edison first began to consider the possibility of an instrument capable of making a graphic record of movement; and on October 17, 1888, he submitted a Caveat which said:

"I am experimenting upon an instrument which does for the eye what the phonograph does for the ear, which is the recording and reproduction of things in motion, and in such a form as to be both cheap and practical and convenient. This apparatus I call a Kinetoscope "Moving View." In the first production of the actual motions that is to say of a continuous Opera, the instrument may be called a Kinetograph, but its subsequent reproduction for which it will be of most use to the public it is properly called a Kinetoscope. The invention consists in photographing continuously a series of pictures occurring at intervals which intervals are greater than eight per second, and photographing these series of pictures in a continuous spiral on a cylinder or plate in the same manner as sound is recorded on the phonograph."

The first motion picture with a story was "The Great Train Robbery" lasting a total of 15 minutes. The Black Maria was Edison's movie studio behind his New Jersey Laboratory. Edison had nine patents with motion pictures.

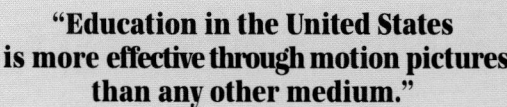

> "Education in the United States is more effective through motion pictures than any other medium."
>
> *Thomas Edison*

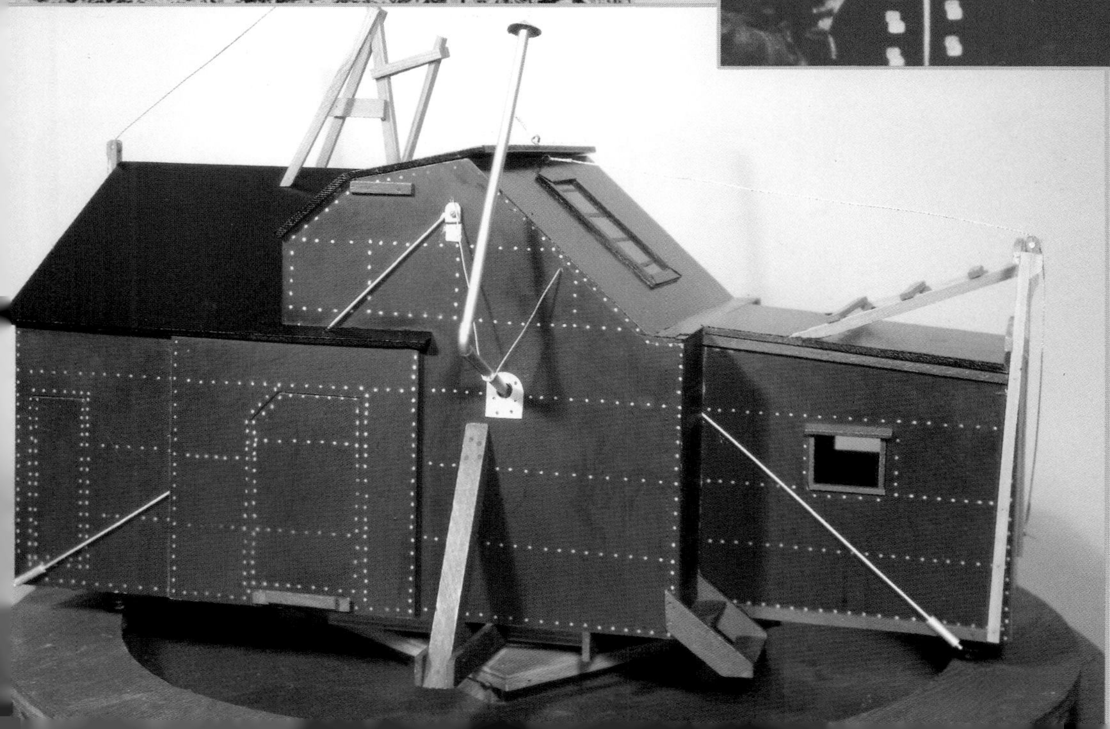

The Edison Battery

With the coming of the automobile, Edison became interested in developing a storage battery that was quickly charged, light weight and both durable and economical. The storage batteries developed at the time were returning only 80% of the power put in. Edison proposed to replace the lead electrodes and acid electrolyte with an alkaline electrolyte with nickel and iron or nickel and cobalt electrodes. In 1909, despite 9,000 failures, seven years of work and over a million dollars spent, Edison finally created a long-lasting alkaline battery which gained wide acceptance for such uses as miner's lamps, telephone and wireless equipment and railroad signal systems. The alkaline battery proved, in the end, to be Edison's most commercially successful product.

Edison's electric launch, Reliance, was kept in a boat house built on the Caloosahatchee River. It provided entertainment and recreation for the family and their many friends. Each of Edison's possessions seemed to serve the dual purpose of providing entertainment and the opportunity for experiments. His launch was no exception. Edison used the boat to test his new nickel-iron-alkaline storage battery. A small generator located on shore provided dockside service for recharging the boat's batteries.

Charles Edison

Governor of New Jersey
Secretary of the Navy

Pictured above is a recreation of Charles Edison's office taken from his home on the 36th floor of the Waldorf-Astoria Towers in New York City. Several of his friends also lived at the Waldorf, including Herbert Hoover and General Douglas MacArthur. Charles, born in 1890, the second of Thomas and Mina's three children, was educated and groomed to take over the Edison Industries. Instead, his life turned to politics. He served as Secretary of Navy under Franklin Roosevelt and as Democratic Governor of New Jersey. Charles Edison passed away on July 31, 1969.

The desk and chair in the office are the ones that served Charles Edison during his stint as Secretary of the Navy. An extensive collection of owls may be seen. Charles collected them as a symbol of wisdom, and his Greenwich Village friends called him a night owl and added to the collection. His distinguished political career included a great deal of constitutional reform and government by investigation.

THE HENRY FORD WINTER ESTATE

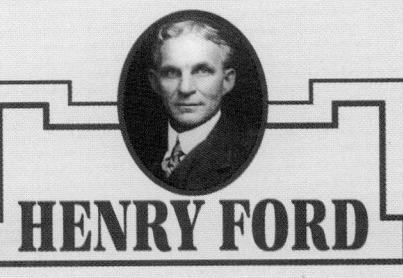

HENRY FORD

The three and one half acre winter estate of Henry Ford was named "The Mangoes" by its original owner for the many mango trees on the property. The house was built in 1911, and Ford purchased it in 1916 for $20,000, enabling him to winter next door to his good friend Edison.

The entrance to the home, which is graced by a bust of Ford, faces majestic, palm-lined McGregor Boulevard. The beautiful greenery and comfortable white wicker furniture were a common sight in Florida homes of the 1920's.

The living room of the home has been authentically restored and looks just as it did when the Fords resided here. The Fords enjoyed evenings of square dancing in this room, moving the furniture to the porch and rolling up the rug. Ford would crank up the Edison phonograph and call the squares.

The Fords had a special love for music. Mrs. Ford was an accomplished musician. She played the piano to entertain family and friends and for her own personal enjoyment. Ford loved the fiddle and often played himself. His love of music inspired Ford to form the Ford Motor Company Band and Henry Ford orchestra. During the 1920's Ford initiated a campaign to revive old-fashioned dancing. His orchestra recorded some of his favorite dance music. He arranged dance classes for friends and Ford executives. He also sponsored music shows which were broadcast on national radio for many years.

The Ford's master bedroom is located above the living room. Clara Ford's dressing room adjoins this room. Clara, an avid needle woman, often found quiet time alone in this cozy room to pursue her sewing or to read a book.

"To find a man who has not benefitted by Edison, and who is not in debt to him, it would be necessary to go deep into the wilderness."

Henry Ford

The upstairs rooms of the Ford home were the exclusive domain of the family. The wide hallway leads to the three room master suite. There is also a spacious family guest room which was frequently used by Ford's son, Edsel. The Fords traveled to Florida in their private railway car. A trunk room on the second floor was used to store the large trunks that accompanied them. The upstairs walls are decorated with nature prints. Ford preferred to surround himself with nature rather than expensive paintings.

Ford and his wife traveled to England in 1912 where Clara became enamored of English furniture, china, and silver. The English walnut Queen Anne style chairs are the perfect compliment to the handmade lace tablecloth. The table is set with Clara's favorite Wedgewood china in the Columbia pattern. A Sheffield silver supper-server adds elegance to the room.

The large sleeping porch adjoining the master bedroom was Henry Ford's favorite spot. A love of nature, acquired while growing up on a farm in Dearborn, Michigan, remained with Ford his entire life. He filled his Florida property with beautiful palm trees, flowers, over 150 citrus trees and a vegetable garden. From the sleeping porch he had a magnificent view of the grounds and his dock on the Caloosahatchee River. Ford loved to fish and spent many afternoons fishing from his dock or the small boat he kept. He was also an avid bird watcher, and this open-air porch was a perfect spot to observe the native birds. He was quite adept at bird calls and sometimes managed to fool his wife with the realistic sounds. The most spectacular view of the river is at sunset, and with this porch the Fords had one of the best seats in town.

Henry Ford was an intensely motivated man. He did not like to be idle. Even while on vacation his mind was on business; and his study, pictured at right, was the perfect place to seclude himself and work quietly on Ford Motor Company business. Mr. Ford visited Fort Myers several years after Edison's death, and rented his home from 1938- 1945 and sold it in August of 1945.

Tribute to a Friend

1847   **1931**

"Mr. Edison was a truly great man. He changed the face of the world in his lifetime, and everything he achieved was beneficial to mankind. The epoch created by his work will influence all the future. His fame is independent of the fluctuating judgements of history; it is etched in light and sound on the daily and hourly life of the world. There was only one Edison."

-Henry Ford

Tribute to a Friend

1847   **1931**

"Thomas Alva Edison did more than any other man to make this world an easier, pleasanter, better world to live in. In him were combined a phenomenal mind, a tremendous energy, and, even up to his declining years, an almost boyish enthusiasm for the successful solving of the problem of the moment. The world has lost one of its greatest men of all time."

- George Eastman

Tribute to a Friend

1847   **1931**

"Mr. Edison had the greatest mind of any man in our generation. His unselfishness, his willingness to sacrifice himself for others, his natural genius combined to drive him on at top speed in his determination to increase the comfort and welfare of the people and to lift human happiness to its highest standard."

-Harvey S. Firestone

HENRY FORD · THOMAS EDISON · HARVEY FIRESTONE

Honors Conferred on Edison

1847   1931

1878 - Doctor of Philosophy, Union College Chevalier of the French Legion of Honor Medal of Superiority, The American Institute (of the City of New York)

1879 - Medals of Excellence, The American Institute

1881 - Diploma of Honor, The General Congress, Paris

1889 - Insignia of a Grand Officer of the Crown of Italy

1892 - The Albert Medal, The British Society of Arts

1904 - Honorary Chief Consulting Engineer, American Institute of Electrical Engineers

1908 - The John Fritz Gold Medal

1913 - Rathenau Gold Medal, The American Museum of Safety

1915 - The Civic Forum Gold Medal Medal of The Franklin Institute Doctor of Science, Princeton University

1916 - Honorary Member of the Illuminating Engineering Society Doctor of Laws, University of the State of New York

1917 - Dedication plaque marking the first electrical central station in New York City

1920 - Distinguished Service Medal, U.S. Navy Department

1923 - Silver replica of the Edison Medal, Engineers Club of New York Honorary Life Member of the Order of Loyal Knights of the Round Table

1925 - Edison pioneers dedicate tablet on the site of Edison's laboratory, Menlo Park, N.J. Medal of Public Instruction, Venezuelan Government

1928 - Gold Medal for Sciences, The Society of Arts and Science October 29, 1928, Congressional Gold Medal

"It is given to few men of any age, nation or calling to become benefactors of all humanity. That distinction came abundantly to Thomas Alva Edison. His lifelong search for truth, fructifying in more than a thousand inventions, made him the greatest inventor our nation has produced, and revolutionized civilization itself. He has been a precious asset to the whole world."

Herbert Hoover, President of the United States